BE A SMART CLIENT

How To Hire The Best Lawyer
And Help Win Your Case

Companion Client Workbooks
available at
www.BeASmartClient.com

Ellen L. Hughes

The McKee Company
www.BeASmartClient.com
P.O. Box 22996, Denver, CO 80222
contact@themckeecompany.com
(303)719-2154
Copyright ©2015 The McKee Company
Ellen L. Hughes

For more resources,
visit www. **BeASmartClient.com**

ISBN-13: 978-1511772297
ISBN-10: 1511772298

Disclaimer

The information contained herein should not be taken as legal advice. The views expressed in this book and the website www.BeASmartClient.com are those of the author alone. The author is not an attorney and has never practiced law.

INTRODUCTION

Throughout my career as a paralegal, I noticed that most problems between client and lawyer were due to poor communication. Misinterpretation, incomplete instructions and false expectations created confusion which resulted in problems that could have been easily avoided.

Be A Smart Client details how to find the right attorney for your needs, which questions to ask and basic instruction that applies to any legal matter. It gives you insight into what to expect and request throughout the entire attorney/client relationship. You will learn the best actions to take in any circumstance to achieve optimal results. Quizzes at the end of each chapter highlight major points.

In any case, how you and your lawyer interact affects the outcome. Take advantage of what this book has to offer, turn the page now to **Be A Smart Client!**

CONTENTS

1

►CHOOSING AN ATTORNEY

1. Picking the right lawyer*

The most important thing is to hire an attorney who meets your legal and personal needs. Advertising is a good way to find many things, but when hiring a lawyer, use a more direct approach. The local bar association is a great resource; they may know attorneys who charge on a sliding scale. Conduct a search on the internet for lawyers with experience in the field covering your needs. Colleagues, friends, and family are good for referrals.

Even though the terms "lawyer" and "attorney" are used interchangeably in daily conversation, technically a lawyer is trained in the law but has not necessarily passed the bar exam. An attorney is trained, passed the exam and admitted to practice law.

2. Determine your needs

What are your personal preferences?

- Do you feel more at ease with a man or a woman? *(There is no hard and fast rule for gender. There are tough men lawyers and mild-mannered female lawyers and vice versa.)*
- Do you prefer working with a younger or older person?
- How far are you willing to travel for appointments?
- How do you prefer to communicate? Phone, e-mail, text or in person
- How involved do you want to be?
- Do you prefer an attorney who is casual or more formal?

3. Initial contact

During the selection process, your first contact should be via telephone. Ask questions to get a feel for their personality and how they work. Some questions to ask:

- Do you have experience with my type of case?
- If so, what is your success rate?
- What is your field of expertise?
- Do you have time to devote to my case?
- How do you prefer to correspond - phone calls, text, letters, e-mails?
- How promptly do you return calls and e-mails?
- Will you keep me regularly informed of actions taken in my case? How often?
- How do you charge - flat fee or contingency fee? (*See #61*)
- What is your attorney registration number? (*See #5*)

Even though an attorney may have worked on your type of case, **it does not mean they are an expert in that field.** Their main expertise may lie elsewhere but for various reasons (*help a friend, additional income, required by firm to accept the case*) they took a case outside their selected field.

4. Reflect on the call

Immediately after the call, think about the conversation. What is your immediate reaction? Was it a good conversation? How do you feel about the attorney? Ask yourself:

- Are they someone I would feel comfortable sharing intimate details of my life?
- Do I feel they will have my best interest at heart?
- Did they answer my questions so I could easily understand them?
- Did they seem to be organized?
- Do I feel they will respect me and my time?

If you answer "no" to any of the above, keep looking until you find one who comes across as confident and makes you feel comfortable.

5. Due diligence

Once you have found at least three attorneys who pass the first round, it's time to dig deeper. Using their name or attorney registration number, check for any complaints lodged against them. Each state keeps records of complaints. Call your state bar association and ask where to find this information.

 BONUS ONLINE CONTENT: Research an attorney's status and disciplinary history by clicking the Find a Lawyer/State Bar Associations tab on www.BeASmartClient.com.

If the attorney's record shows no history of grievances, it is time to set an appointment.

DO YOU REMEMBER?

1. Where can you find attorneys working on a sliding fee scale?

2. Who keeps data on attorneys who have complaints filed against them?

3. List five questions to ask yourself to determine your personal preferences when hiring a lawyer.

4. Name three outside sources you can ask for an attorney referral.

2

▶ THE INITIAL APPOINTMENT

6. Be Prepared

The first meeting is a fact-finding mission. This is the time to tell the attorney what you want and determine if they can deliver it. Don't feel pressured to make an immediate decision.

Be specific when describing what you want.

- *I am seeking a divorce and I want the house, car and ferret.*
- *I want to file a slander lawsuit for $50,000.*
- *I want a simple will drawn up within 30 days.*
- *I want my company switched from a sole proprietor to an LLC.*

Offer some specifics about your case so the attorney can make an informed assessment. Include your thoughts and any feedback from people who have your best interest at heart. Compile it in logical order. Make sure to **answer the 5 W's - Who, What, When, Where and Why.** A construction defect case may look like this:

Who: Contractor's Name
What: I want to sue the Contractor for $_____ because the new siding started pulling away from the house and exposed the interior of the house to the elements. The cost of the siding was $_____ and items inside the house were damaged.
When: I noticed the damage within three months of installation.
Where: My house at 123 Main Street, Springville, IA.
Why: I want to get enough money to fix the problem and cover household items ruined by the defective siding.

This way you your attorney will get a complete understanding of what you want and why you want it.

7. A good first impression

Many attorneys offer a free initial consultation. Schedule one at a time convenient for you. Arrive on time, bring your list (*See #6*) and any pertinent legal and personal documents. Bring a picture ID. <u>Don't bring children or pets</u>. Call ahead to ask about parking. Dress appropriately. If you aren't sure what to wear, ask. Dressing in ripped, dirty clothes or looking like you just rolled out of bed sends a message you aren't serious about your case. If you don't think it is important, why should anyone else?

8. Ask questions

Do they think your case has merit? Do they have special training that might apply in your situation? Asking questions and weighing the answers help you make informed decisions. Other questions to ask:

- In your opinion, what is the best case scenario?
- What is the worst?
- What is a realistic outcome?
- Would you pursue this if you were me? Why or why not?
- Is this region sympathetic to my type of case? (*See #60*)
- What is a reasonable amount of time and costs I should expect?

When deciding on the questions to ask, use the basic Who, What, When, Where and Why. If you want a will drawn up quickly, ask if they can do it within the requested timeframe and their charge. (*I know someone who was kept waiting over a year for a simple will.*) Your questions will depend on the legal matter. Is there a deadline for filing? Do you want specific restitution? Let the attorney know the basic information. Once they know your expectations, they may offer options you had not considered.

9. Listen to <u>how</u> they talk

- Are their answers hard to follow?
- Do they use legal jargon?
- Do they answer a question with a question?
- Do they change the subject?
- Do they brag or oversell their services?

These are red flags. If they evade questions in the first meeting, what is going to happen down the road?

There are times when a client inquires about the status of their case and the lawyer responds by: 1) peppering the client with unneeded questions, or 2) assigning them busywork to the point they are too overwhelmed to think about what the attorney is doing - or not doing. Avoid this kind of attorney.

10. Intimidation factor

Attorneys can be intimidating and people may feel pressured to hire the first one. Don't be tempted.

The first meeting is a fact-finding mission. While they are assessing your case, you should be assessing them. Meet with at least three lawyers before making a decision. Take notes to review later at home.

11. Trust your instincts

This meeting is to determine if you can work with the attorney. If you feel tension or something doesn't feel right, thank the attorney for their time and let them know you will get back to them. As soon as possible, preferably the same day, let them know you won't need their services.

12. Take a friend

This is wise, especially if you are ill, on medication, or feeling out of sorts. A second person may catch things you miss or think of other questions to ask. Compare notes afterwards.

If you feel the attorney is the right one and want to hire them on the spot, ask to confer with your friend in private before making a decision.

13. The waiting room

If your appointment is for 10:30 and you are not seen until 11:00, that is a red flag. It could mean the lawyer: 1) does not value your time, 2) isn't organized, or 3) overbooks clients. This is not a good way to start a relationship. If they give a plausible explanation, give them another chance. If no reason is offered, move on to the next name on your list. It has been my experience that lawyers rarely, if ever, apologize so do not expect one.

14. A revolving door

If you interview an lawyer who can't seem to keep help, take heed. An office in a constant state of flux speaks volumes - none of it good. Not only does it point out possible personality problems, but the very structure of the office (*including your file*) can be affected. (*I know an attorney who went through five*

13

paralegals in one year.) Who suffers most when this happens? The client!

It is easy to gauge the office atmosphere. Pay attention to how employees relate and talk to each other. When you speak to the staff, ask how long they worked there.

DO YOU REMEMBER?

1. Name four actions that can increase the success of your first appointment.

2. Why should you take someone with you to appointments?

3. Why should you listen to how an attorney talks and not just what they say?

4. How long should you wait before let an attorney know you don't need their services?

3

►THE HIRING PROCESS

You found an attorney who seems to fit your needs. Now what? Good communication is key, during the hiring process and throughout your whole case.

15. Discuss your expectations

You have already made your basic needs known. Now it is time to give details. The lawyer is not a mind reader; give them as much information as possible. The best course of action to take is get the companion workbook. (*See Page 93*) Let them know what you expect - not only the outcome you desire, but how you want to be treated. What level of service do you expect? How often do you want updates? The

Client Constitution covers billing, communication, and personnel issues which you should discuss and agree on <u>before</u> hiring any attorney.

16. Client Constitution

Review each point thoroughly and choose ones that are important to you. Discuss them with your lawyer. Make sure they agree to your requests. If they don't agree with one that is important to you, find an attorney who will.

<u>The Client Constitution</u>

- Client prefers to communicate with the same personnel throughout the case.
- If staffing changes occur, Client will not pay for time to educate new attorneys/staff about the case.
- Client will be kept current on all case developments in a timely manner.

- Client will be copied on all court-filed documents immediately after filing.
- Client will be copied on all correspondence in relation to case.
- Client will be provided a schedule in advance with all court-appointed due dates (*depositions, discovery*).
- Photocopying may not exceed 15¢ per page (*or local average rate*). If there is a large volume of documents, Client shall be given the opportunity to shop around for price comparison.
- Client shall receive copies of invoices/receipts for items charged by outside vendors (*copies, postage, private investigator, etc.*).
- Before incurring any expense over $_____ (*not less than $25*), Client will be notified for approval.
- Before ordering medical or other records, attorney will verify

insurance or other assets to cover cost. (*See #58*)

- Before dismissing a case, attorney will notify Client. (*See #37*)
- Hourly rates may not be increased without prior Client approval.
- Client will receive a monthly statement detailing description, timekeeper, time and costs.
- Client shall receive copies of all invoices/receipts for items charged by outside vendors.
- Amounts submitted by outside vendors will be charged to Client at face value.
- Client will receive prompt follow-up to all communications to attorney and staff.
- Client expects efficient, timely completion of work, including keeping Client file current and in good order.
- Meetings are held during regular office hours unless cleared in advance with Client.

- Only one lawyer and/or staff member will attend meetings, hearings or other matters on Client's behalf.
- Attorney in charge will avoid:
  ○ Overstaffing
  ○ Frequent shuffling of assigned personnel
  ○ Extensive rework of a written work product
  ○ Handling specific tasks by persons who are either overqualified or underqualified
  ○ Review of documents by multiple timekeepers
  ○ Performing premature or minor legal or factual research
- Client will not be billed for:
  ○ Internal conferences
  ○ Internal notes or memorandum
  ○ Scheduling meetings or depositions
  ○ Research regarding simple issues which should already be within the knowledge of the attorney
  ○ Timekeeping (*billing for time it takes to create the bill*)

BONUS ONLINE CONTENT: Visit www.BeASmartClient.com for more questions to ask an attorney.

Once you have discussed the Client Constitution with your attorney, record that it has been discussed. If possible, have the attorney sign a copy. Send a copy of it to them, with a short cover letter, *"I am sending you a copy of the Client Constitution that we discussed on (date)"*. Keep a copy of both for your files.

Do you feel you are overstepping your authority by telling your attorney what you expect? Don't. Corporations do it all the time. It's just good business. There is nothing in the Client Constitution that demands too much or is out of line with what a client should expect from their attorney. Discussing and agreeing upon these issues in the beginning increases your odds of having a harmonious attorney/client relationship.

17. Business Owners

The Client Constitution is suitable for individuals and companies. However, there are additional points that apply more specifically to business owners or clients with action-intensive cases.

- Messenger services should be provided at cost and used only when an alternative is unavailable.
- Express mail should be provided at cost and used only when an alternate service is not available.
- Client needs to approve all travel expenses in advance.
- No local travel expenses (*within 100 miles of attorney's office*) will be reimbursed.

18. Level of involvement

No one has a more vested interest in your case than you. *Decide how hands-on you want to be.* At one end of the spectrum you can be very involved and offer to do research and legwork that doesn't require legal training. *(This level is usually allowed only by small firms or a solo attorney.)* On the opposite end, you can take a *laissez faire* approach and let the attorney and staff perform all the work.

At the very minimum, keep all paperwork organized in one place so you can easily find any document. An expandable file folder works well. It is also good to track due dates on a calendar so you know the deadlines. *(Companion Workbooks include blank tables to easily journal all important information - see Page 95)* No matter your level of involvement, don't overstep your authority or become a nuisance. **When in doubt, ask your attorney.**

19. Fee agreement
Once you decide on a lawyer, they will give you a fee agreement to sign. <u>Read it carefully</u>. It is a contract covering the actions the lawyer offers to do for you, terms of payment and your acceptance of the

terms. It is signed by both parties. Depending on the type of case and how detailed the agreement (*See #61*), it may describe how fees will be set, what expenses will be paid, if a retainer fee is required and how the funds will be replenished. In a contingency case, it will specify the attorney's percentage and when fees will be calculated.

 BONUS ONLINE CONTENT: Review examples of different types of fee agreements at www.BeASmartClient.com

DO YOU REMEMBER?

1. Who signs the fee agreement?

2. If you choose the minimum amount of participation, what is the very least action you should take?

3. Why you should want to be involved in your case?

4. What points in the Client Constitution are important to you?

5. How can you record the fact that you have discussed the Client Constitution with the attorney?

4

▶ BE A MODEL CLIENT

You have hired an attorney who meets your requirements. Now it's time to talk about what they expect from you.

20. Client responsibilities

DO...

...Respond to all communication from attorney in a timely manner.

...Keep messages short and to the point.

...Dress appropriately for all meetings and/or court dates.

...Tell your attorney everything.

...Carefully read all documents your attorney gives you.

...Keep all paperwork organized.

...Keep a record of documents you give to attorney. (*See Page 95*)

...Make sure your attorney has your current contact information.

...Provide copies of all documents your attorney requests and <u>keep the original</u> (*unless requestes.*)

...Pay your bill on time.

...Let your attorney know as soon as possible if you will be late or cannot make an appointment.

DO NOT...

...Leave repeated messages about the same issue.

...Leave several messages in one day (*unless it is an emergency*). It is better to consolidate them into one message.

...Lie.

...Show up at the office without an appointment.

...Bring children or pets to meetings.

...Get personally involved with your attorney.

...Contact witnesses or others involved in your case without first informing attorney.

In addition to these rules, treat your attorney as you want to be treated - with respect and common courtesy.

21. Respect staff

Employees are an important part of the legal team. A client may talk to them more often than the lawyer. If you have a legal question, speak to the attorney. If you need documents or a question that doesn't require legal expertise, speak to a staff member. Show the staff the same courtesy and respect as you do the lawyer. Do not leave multiple messages regarding the same issue, keep to the point and be polite.

22. Assist the attorney

Depending how involved you want to be, your comfort level and agreement with your attorney, there are several ways you can assist.

- **Offer to do research** that does not require legal training. A lot can be done on the internet. (*See #67, #68*)

- **Pick up and deliver** documents or copy jobs, especially if they are needed immediately. It can save the cost of a rush fee (*which you ultimately pay*).
- **Obtain contact information** for friends and family who are potential witnesses. ***Inform the attorney before you do this*** in case they have a reason for you not to contact them.

Small firms and sole practitioners are more open to client involvement than a larger firm. Whatever assistance you offer, keep a record of your actions with as many details as possible.

23. Inside an attorney's mind

Wouldn't it be helpful to know how an attorney thinks? It might make it easier to understand their actions. In her book, *Lawyer, Know Thyself*, Susan Daicoff discusses the personality traits of an attorney:

"Individuals who choose to enter law school seem to generally share the following characteristics as children: They are highly focused on academics, have greater needs for dominance, leadership and attention and they prefer initiating activity...It was found, in a comparative study, that concern for emotional suffering and for the feelings of others tended to be less emphasized than in the childhood homes of dental or social work students."

In short - they are logical, focused, like to be in charge, and seek attention.

Like Mr. Spock from Star Trek, attorneys can be perceived as cold and unemotional. They deal with facts. They are logical. They do not deal well with people who are emotional so save the drama for friends and family.

24. Get your point across

When talking with an attorney, it may appear they are so focused on what <u>they</u> are saying, they don't hear <u>you</u>. If you have something to say, wait for a break then get their attention. Look them in the eye, clear your throat, tap a pencil - anything to make them focus on what you are saying. Remember, lawyers love to talk so let them to a point but be vigilant and say what you need to say. If they charge by the hour, guide them back to the current topic as soon as possible.

25. Confidence builders

There are many easy ways to build up your confidence so you feel more in control.

- Imagine wearing a cape like Superman's or having a crown or tiara on your head. It may sound silly, but these mental images can make you feel and act powerful and important. Prefer another image? Choose one that makes you feel strong.

- Present yourself in the best possible light. The cost of your outfit is not important; what is key is that you appear confident in both manner and dress.

- Increase your energy. Tapping on the K-27 acupressure points just before your appointment will help you feel more alert. Place your fingers on your collarbone, slide them toward the center and find the bumps where they stop. Drop about an inch beneath these corners and slightly outward. Most people have a slight indent here. Gently tap or massage these points while breathing deeply (*in through the nose and out through the mouth*) for about 20 seconds. This makes your energy flow in the right direction and helps you think more clearly.

- Increase your personal space. Instead of keeping your body and belongings directly in front of you, spread out a little bit. Without being overly dramatic, drape an arm over the chair next to you. Place your belongings on the table instead of on the floor. Take up more space (*not a lot*) than you normally would.

- Try this at a restaurant: First keep your belonging in a small space, close together. Then spread out a little bit and notice if there is a difference in how the wait staff treats you. This has been tested. People who take up more space are perceived as being more important and treated accordingly.

- Keep eye contact. One of the first signs that people are nervous is they find it hard to maintain eye contact. They look at the floor, their hands, the table, anywhere but at the person who is talking to them. Start practicing so you can look the lawyer in the eyes and not flinch. Don't stare, but smile, blink and pay attention to what they are saying. You will come across as confident.

26. Control or manipulation?

You want an attorney who is in control; someone who will take charge and guide the outcome to benefit you. It is when they try to manipulate you that problems arise. They may ask a question in such a way that you feel obligated to give a specific answer (*like a salesman*). Or perhaps they ask you to do something you consider unreasonable. If you feel this happening, ask yourself:

- How will this help my case?
- Is this in line with what we agreed upon in the Client Constitution?
- What would happen if I do or don't do this?
- Are there other options?

Review the options and if you still feel it is not in your best interest, tell them the issue has been addressed and there will be no further discussion on this point unless they offer new information.

DO YOU REMEMBER?

1. Name five responsibilities of a client.

2. Should you give the attorney your original documents or copies?

3. What are different ways you can help with your case?

4. What are four characteristics of an attorney?

5. What should you do if you feel you are being manipulated?

5

►END THE RELATIONSHIP

When all is said and done, hopefully everyone walks away happy. You have your desired outcome and the attorney gets paid. Wrapping up is fairly simple. The attorney gives you a document outlining any final matters they need to take care of and/or any action you need to take or verbally tells you.

But what if it doesn't end well? Or you feel you need to get a new attorney? Does the thought of firing an attorney scare you? It shouldn't. If you hired a plumber and they didn't show up for two weeks, you would have no problem firing them. Firing a lawyer is no different. However, there are a few things to consider before giving them the pink slip. A few precautions can alleviate future problems.

27. Talk with them

Before terminating your attorney's services, it is in your best interest to talk with them. If you think they aren't giving your case their full attention, talk to them about it. It may be simple miscommunication. If the problem appears to be overbilling, it could be an accounting error. Try to give them the benefit of the doubt. A 10-minute phone call can save a lot of time and headaches.

28. Timing is everything

You can change attorneys at any time but before doing so, consider the consequences. Changing counsel may delay your case. If you must get a new attorney, do it as soon as possible. If you wait until just before trial or some other deadline, it may be hard to find someone willing to take over at that late date.

29. Attorney inaction

Do you feel your attorney has lost interest in your case? Are they not returning phone calls or not keeping you up to date? (*You did discuss the Client Constitution, right?*) Before giving them the axe, express your concerns by sending a simple, factual, non-emotional email or letter. If they don't respond or address your issues satisfactorily, then it is time to sever ties.

30. Get a second opinion

If you feel the problem is deeper than a personality conflict or simple disagreement, talk to someone. **Do not mention your attorney's name** or information that would make it easy to determine their identity. *Follow this rule especially when talking in public or on your cell phone.* You could be opening yourself up for a lawsuit. Consider talking to an attorney in the same legal field. Ask them to evaluate your lawyer's actions.

31. Contact bar association

The local bar association is a vast source of information. Without revealing your lawyer's name or firm name, relate your situation. They will not give legal advice, but they can determine if your attorney's actions are problematic.

32. Personal reasons

Maybe you want to stop the action due to personal reasons. You decide not to sell your business, you and your spouse kiss and make up, the lawsuit is taking over your life. Whatever the reason, you have made the decision to stop and not go forward. Just be sure it is in your best interest and no one is forcing the decision on you.

33. Drop or postpone?

If your case involves a lawsuit, talk to your attorney on how the case is progressing and any options before dropping it. Ask if there is a statute of limitations in case you decide to file later. (*See #54*)

34. You are entitled to your file

You have decided to sever ties with your attorney. What should you reasonably expect? First, you are entitled to a copy of your file *minus work product.* Work product consists of an attorney's private conversations, research, notes, writings, and other confidential materials. You are entitled to copies of any depositions if you paid for them.

The attorney may charge to copy your file. Review your fee agreement for details regarding this. Since you should have been already copied on all documents filed with the court and all correspondence, the number of documents you need may be few.

35. Monies due you

If you paid a retainer, the balance should be returned to you with your file or soon thereafter. The refund should include an overview of total fees and costs. Check this with your detailed monthly statements. If you owe money, the attorney should release your file after payment is made.

36. Arbitration and Mediation

In place of a trial, you can request **arbitration** where parties bring their dispute before a neutral third-party, an arbitrator. They are often former judges or experienced attorneys. Once both parties have presented their evidence, the arbitrator issues a decision which is legally binding. On the other hand, in **mediation,** the mediator needs no formal legal training. They make suggestions which the parties can accept or reject.

 BONUS ONLINE CONTENT: If you have decided to file a grievance, visit www.BeASmartClient.com for state bar association contact information.

37. When to report an attorney

Missing filing deadlines, failing to advise you of court dates or suggesting you lie are considered unethical and should be reported to the bar association. Other examples of conduct that may be cause for discipline:

- They represent the other party, whether in your case or another
- Misrepresent whether or not they have taken certain actions
- Will not provide a complete written accounting for money due you or money they hold on your behalf
- Settle your case without your permission and nothing in the fee agreement authorizes them to do so

To file a grievance, contact your local bar association. Find details at www.BeASmartClient.com

38. Filing a grievance

When filing a grievance, be certain of the facts. You need proof; gut feelings or intuition won't stand up in court. You must be able to provide evidence, either with documentation or witnesses. Filing a grievance does not guarantee the attorney will be sanctioned but it should at least make someone sit up and take notice.

DO YOU REMEMBER?

1. After ending your case, do you have to pay to get your file?

2. Why should you not mention your attorney's name when talking to others regarding possible bad behavior?

3. List five actions a lawyer may take that can be considered unethical?

4. What could happen if you change attorneys close to trial?

6

►TO-DO LIST

The key is to leave a paper trail. The more documentation and details, the better. Be thorough. You don't know what will be the "smoking gun" that could make or break your case.

39. The devil is in the details

The actions you take depend on the matter. If you need a business contract drawn up, your involvement will be negligible. If you were injured in an auto accident and are seeking restitution, your to-do list may seem never-ending. Attorneys should tell you what they need but sometimes things fall through the cracks. The steps that follow are geared toward a *personal injury lawsuit* and is extensive.

Much of this work can be done prior to hiring an attorney. If your matter is less complicated, follow only the steps that apply to you.

The Client Workbook is excellent for keeping all aspects of your case in one place. (*See Page 95*)

40. Keep a diary

Start a daily diary as soon as possible. The longer you put it off, the more details you forget. If you aren't able to write or type, have someone else write it or record it and have it transcribed later.

Start your diary with a complete narrative of the incident. List as many details as you can.

▶ Date
▶ Location *(address & description)*
▶ People/animals description of all involved
▶ Contact information of witnesses
▶ Vehicle license plate, signage, bumper stickers, condition, etc.

▶ <u>Time</u> of day
▶ <u>Weather</u> conditions

Once you start your diary, keep it current. *Enter notes on everything, whether or not you think it is important.* You can determine later what is pertinent. What belongs in your diary? Your conversations, thoughts, and actions.

Conversations
Any time you talk with anyone involving your incident, record the following:

▶ First and last name of all participants
▶ Person's occupation and/or relationship to your case *(medical provider, witness, mechanic)*
▶ Complete contact details *(name, phone, address, e-mail)*
▶ Date
▶ Time and duration *(include a.m. or p.m.)*
▶ Location *(via telephone, e-mail, or address, if you met in person)*

▶ Subject of discussion (*include details and direct quotes when possible*)

You want to paint a vivid picture, include as many details as possible.

Thoughts
Keep track of your feelings.

▶ Your mood (*happy, depressed, sad, angry*)
▶ What caused you to feel this way. (*Sad because I cannot attend a wedding due to my injuries. Afraid because I cannot pay my bills*)

You want people to understand your frame of mind.

Actions
Keep track of your day-to-day life and how it has changed.

▶ Events that are a direct result (*doctor appointments*)

▶ Things you cannot do any more (*morning walks, laundry, mowing*)
▶ How your injuries affect daily life (*can't sit for long periods of time*)

Show specifically how your life has changed as a direct result of the incident.

41. Contact list

Keep contact details in one place. Some information may already be in your diary but also <u>keep a separate file</u>. It will be easier to retrieve quickly when needed. *Group your contacts according to their relation to your case* - witnesses, medical providers, etc. For people you contact often, store their number in your cell phone or on speed dial. Anything that saves you time can save your sanity. **Keep the list current.** Do not delete people you have contacted but no longer work at the company; note them as "inactive." You still may need to contact them.

Include assistants and support staff in your contact list. They can be invaluable. When an attorney, doctor or other professional is unavailable, the assistant may be able to locate them or answer your question.

Strive to include the following for each contact:

Name
Telephone (Main)
Telephone (Other)
Street Address
Mailing Address
Email
Company
Occupation (*doctor or assistant, lawyer or paralegal, etc.*)
Relationship to case (*health provider, witness, etc.*)
Hours/Days they are available
Comments

42. Record your impressions

Get in the habit of recording your _impression_ of a person. Notes like "helpful" or "had an accident similar to mine" will come in handy if you need to contact them again. It helps you establish rapport and they will be more inclined to help you. If you felt they could not help or were not the right person to talk to, make a note so you will not waste your time with them again. *The more you record, the fewer things you have to remember.*

43. Calendar future dates

A diary keeps track of the past; a calendar keeps track of the future. An example of something to track on your calendar: "If I have not heard from Mr. Jones by today, send Letter #2" *(See #49)*. "If I have not received report by today, contact attorney."

Attorneys keep track of dates with a process called "calendaring". Ask your attorney to share court dates with you so you can **record them on your calendar**. This may seem unnecessary, especially if you don't want to be kept in the loop. But there have been cases where attorneys missed deadlines for deposition and/or filing documents with the court. *(See #37)* These errors negatively impact the case. If a due date is approaching and you haven't received notice that action has been taken, call your attorney and ask for a status report.

44. Track loss of income

Your attorney should provide you with a log to keep track of income and expenses but that doesn't always happen. **It is up to you to keep accurate records**. If you missed work due to injuries, keep a record of your days absent. If you are employed by someone, it is easy to keep track of missed work.

If you are self-employed, get in the habit of keeping detailed notes regarding your business schedule. Did you miss a meeting due to a doctor appointment? Were you unable to give a seminar which could have resulted in new contacts or income? Make a note of it.

As with the contact list, this information will be in your diary but also *keep a separate log strictly for lost income* so it will be easier to find when needed. A simple table like the one below is sufficient.

Date	Income	Reason
		Description of lost opportunity to make money and/or contacts for future earnings

45. Keep all receipts

Medical and legal expenses are easy to remember, but expand your thinking. If an injury prevents you from performing some task, keep track of money you paid to get it done (*mowing, cleaning, laundry, etc.*). Do you chug Pepto Bismol because the antibiotics you have to take are eating up your stomach? Unable to use your paid gym membership due to your injuries?

Keep a running total so it will be easy to know your out-of-pocket expenses at a glance. If the receipt doesn't include a description, write it on the receipt. Your expense log might look like this:

Date	Amount	Payee and Description
1/2/12	$15.45	CVS - Antibiotics
1/2/12	$ 1.80	Postage - original signed documents to attorney
1/4/12	$ 8.25	20 miles - Trip to doctor - gas, parking

46. Track communication

In addition to daily events, keep records of any communication regarding the incident in your diary. This includes telephone calls, e-mails, texts, letters and in-person conversations. Keep copies of any attachments to correspondence.

>Telephone calls are easy to track, especially if you use a cell phone. Make a note of the day and time, who you talked to and the subject of the call. A detailed diary holds a lot of weight in court. Recording a conversation can be done, but check your local laws. Each state has wiretapping laws. When something regarding a date or specific action is discussed, follow it up with something in writing to the other person which reiterates what was said. It can be as simple as a short e-mail: *"As we discussed on the phone today, you will send me your findings on Mr. Smith by Wednesday, the 23rd."*

>**Written correspondence** leaves a paper trail and is important in any lawsuit. Keep copies of all letters you send and receive, *along with any attachments*. Most letters may be sent via U.S. Mail. If you send something requiring an answer or original documents, **require the recipient sign for it**. Many private delivery companies offer this service (*FedEx, UPS*). The U.S. Post Office offers Certified Mail with Return Receipt Requested. This also allows you to track the package and know when it is delivered and who signed for it.

47. Basic communication rules

Include your contact information on everything. The placement doesn't matter - it can be at the top in the letterhead or under your signature. This applies to all forms of communication. Include a subject line that provides enough details so the recipient can determine the matter at a glance. Include items like name, account or case number, date of loss and name of defendant. (*See example below*)

Address
City, State and Zip Code
Email Address
Phone Number(s)

Date

Address

Re: Your Name
        Case No.: 12345
        Date of Loss: 7/26/11
        Defendant: Individual's Name

Dear (Mr./Mrs. Name or Sir/Madam):

Body of letter

Sincerely,

Your Name

Enclosures - *List all enclosures*

cc: *List all who are receiving a copy*
bcc: *List all who are receiving a copy but
        you don't want others to know they
        are receiving it. The bcc is not written
        on the original letter, only on your
        copy.*

---

48. Tracking e-mails

When sending an e-mail, keep a copy for yourself so you have a dated copy for your files. Create an email folder and move all emails in it to find them quickly. Every time you send an email, *change the subject line to reflect the content.* For instance, if the lawyer emails you to ask if you approve an expenditure, the subject line in your reply should say something like "Answer for expenditure for expert witness." A **clearly defined subject line** makes it is easy to find a specific email.

49. Mass produce letters

Usually the lawyer contacts companies, but if you are dealing with businesses before hiring a lawyer, there are steps you can take to make the process easier. If there is a business that is hard to deal with (*insurance companies are a prime example*), use the original letter as a template to write future letters. If the company does not take action after the first one, use the original letter with the first paragraph referring to the previous letter.

"I am writing because I have not received a response to my letter of January 31, 2013."

Copy and paste the rest of the original letter here.

If you are corresponding by e-mail, use the prior e-mail to create a new one, and make reference to the previous email.

50. Get to the point

In all correspondence, state the facts clearly and succinctly. Do not be emotional. Do not use profanity. Get to the point immediately. Instead of writing "That rude employee said he would send me the paperwork but didn't," write, "*I am still waiting for the paperwork Mr. Jones promised to send when we talked at 2:15 p.m. on May 15.*"

51. Allow time to reply

If you don't receive a response to the first letter, how long should you wait before sending the next one? You don't want them to forget about you yet not come across as a stalker. A good rule of thumb, *if you haven't received a response within two weeks, send the next letter.*

52. Take it to the next level

What if you don't get a response? Go up the chain of command. Give people two chances to reply. Then contact their supervisor. If you still don't get satisfaction, contact someone above them. And so on. If you have to go to the top and contact the head of the company, so be it. They won't be happy to hear a complaint about poor customer service and will want the situation handled quickly. (*You may want to go directly to the owner of the company or manager of the department. It saves a lot of time.*)

DO YOU REMEMBER?

1. List five items on your to-do list.

2. When should you require a delivery receipt?

3. How long should you wait before sending a follow-up letter?

4. When a lawyer "calendars," what does this mean?

5. Why should you keep separate contact and income logs?

6. What should you do if a receipt doesn't have a description on it?

7. What three types of things should you track in your diary?

8. What five items should your contact information include?

Be A Smart Client

7

►THE BASICS

While behavior varies from attorney to attorney and case to case, there are basic fundamentals that apply across the board. *Learn these* and you will save time, money and your sanity. *Follow them* and you will be your own best advocate.

53. Keep your eyes on the prize

Always have your goal in mind. If you want to file a lawsuit for $5,000 and the attorney's fees will run that much or more, it's time to rethink things. Do you need a simple drawn up? The cost and time should be minimal so if your lawyer seems to be taking an inordinate amount of time to complete it, it is time to ask questions. A general timeframe should have already been established. (*See #8*) When deciding whether to go forward, consider how much money and time you are willing to spend. Also ask yourself: *Is it worth the aggravation?*

54. Statute of limitations
Maybe you are undecided if you want to go forward with your case. There are many reasons to put things on hold; just be aware there is a deadline for filing a lawsuit.

The deadline is known as the *statute of limitations*. For personal injury cases, this can run anywhere from one to six years from the date of the incident; for property damage it is one to ten years. Each state sets their own time limit. Check with your state bar association or call an attorney who practices in that field of law for deadline information.

 BONUS ONLINE CONTENT: For state bar agency contact information, visit www.BeASmartClient.com

55. Be prepared for anything

Assume nothing will be easy. Act as if you are dealing with a large company or the government. Some people will argue that this type of negative thinking is wrong. I say it is being practical. If you think everything will go smoothly and it does not, it makes it harder to rally yourself after a letdown. If you expect it is going to be an uphill battle, you steel yourself against adversity. Then even the smallest triumph makes you feel like a winner.

56. No insurance

What if the person responsible for your loss has no insurance or personal assets to attach? Personal injury attorneys work almost exclusively on cases that have a pot of gold at the end of the rainbow. No rainbow. No pot. No attorney. Ads portraying altruistic lawyers show only part of the picture. For lawyers to truly care, the defendant or their insurance company has to have deep pockets. ***There has to be money to make it worth their time***.

57. Realistic timeline

Television attorneys wrap up a case in 60 minutes. Real cases can take years. Discovery alone (*depositions, interrogatories, obtaining records,*) can take months, even years, to gather. Lawsuits for personal injury cases may not be filed until an expert has declared the person to be as healthy as they are going to get, known as Maximum Medical Improvement (MMI).

For non-litigious matters such as a patent search or estate planning, the timeline is much shorter. Ask your attorney how many hours they anticipate it will take. *You play an important role here.* The quicker you provide information, the faster the attorney can complete the work.

58. Wait to order records

Ask your attorney to verify the availability of insurance or assets before ordering medical or other records. These records can cost thousands of dollars, a bill you ultimately pay. You want to make sure the monetary award will be large enough to justify the expense.

59. Judge versus jury

Only 4%-5% of personal injury cases in the U. S. go to trial; the rest are settled beforehand. Ninety percent of personal injury cases that go to trial are lost. If you are one that make it to trial, request a judge. ***Cases do better when the case is in front of a trial judge*** *rather that a jury.*

60. Awards vary by state

Where you live makes a difference. For example, Colorado is ranked 48th in awarding punitive damages. People still consider Colorado the "Wild West" so when something bad happens, they are supposed to "tough it out." *Translation*: Cases settle for less here than almost any other state.

61. Attorney fees

There are four types of payment plans:

- Hourly rate
- Flat fee
- Retainer
- Contingent fees

Charging by the hour is the most common form of payment. Hourly fees are dependent on the location, size of law firm and experience of the attorney. An attorney with a large firm in a major metropolitan city can charge anywhere from $200 to $600 an hour; a small-town attorney may charge $100 to $200; a lawyer who specializes in specific areas of law can command up to $1,000 an hour.

•**Flat fees** are charged when the case is simple and well defined. Examples of flat fee cases are simple wills, bankruptcy or an uncontested divorce.

●A **retainer** is an advance payment on an hourly rate case. The retainer is held in a trust account held by the attorney and fees and costs are deducted from it. If a retainer is depleted before the case closes, the lawyer requests additional money before continuing work.

●When working on a **contingent fee** basis, the attorney takes no money in advance and gets paid from the money awarded. Examples of contingency cases are automobile accidents and other personal injury cases, medical malpractice and debt collection. Contingent fees are usually 33-1/3% if it doesn't go to trial; 40% if it does.

62. Handling life changes

If you suffer a permanent injury, you may have to alter how you use your body. You cannot change that, but you can control how you react. You may have to make some adaptations, but humans are good at that. Take as much time as you need, but try to move forward every day, even if it is a little bit. Things will get better. (*See #87*)

63. No comparison

Your situation is unique. There are always going to be people who have it worse than you and others who have it better. Do not compare your situation to others. Concentrate on what is best for you. *You cannot direct the wind, but you can adjust your sails.* Control what you can and let go of the rest.

64. The mouth that roared

Most people desire to be friendly. However, **sometimes people equate being friendly with being weak.** A pleasant demeanor may not be advantageous in certain situations. Say, for example, an agency won't release documents necessary to your case. Take a cue from the movie *We Bought A Zoo.* Matt Damon said: "*You know, sometimes all you need is twenty* *seconds of insane courage."* Screw up your courage, turn up the volume and make yourself heard. Don't swear, be obnoxious, or threaten. Don't feel like you can do that? Invite a friend who will make your requests known without being rude.

65. Civil and criminal cases

In personal injury lawsuits, there is a possibility of two cases - criminal and civil.

A criminal case is tried by a public attorney and sues the defendant for any law or ordinance violated during the commission of the incident. It covers out-of-pocket expenses (*medical, prescriptions, co-pays, wages for people hired to do things you are unable to do - laundry, mow lawn, run errands, cook meals, etc.*) It **does not allow** money awarded to be dismissed through bankruptcy.

A civil case is filed by a private attorney **hired by the plaintiff.** It covers **loss of income and pain and suffering** and allows money awarded to **be dismissed through bankruptcy**. A person's income cannot be garnished in a civil case.

DO YOU REMEMBER?

1. You have a better chance of taking your case in front of: a) jury b) judge c) TV court.

2. What is an easy way to find out what the statute of limitations is in your state and for your type of case?

3. Why is it a good idea to plan for the worst and hope for the best?

4. Name three differences between civil and criminal cases.

5. What is meant when a lawyer charges on a contingent basis?

8

▶RESEARCH OPTIONS

In most cases, the attorney and staff will do all the research. However, there are good reasons for you to try your hand at it. Conducting your own research can save you money and time. It can confirm facts or expose bad information. Maybe you want to check into things before you hire an attorney. In my case, the investigator had a lot of incorrect information so by sharing my findings, it cut down on billable hours. And the best news is there are many resources available - **most of them are free.**

What type of research can you do? It depends on what the attorney is comfortable allowing you to do.

66. Background check

This report contains many details that can be used to ferret out other information. Your attorney can order one or you can request a report yourself. There are many websites offering this service. A background report may include:

- Subject's name and former names, such as maiden name
- Social Security Number
- Date of birth
- Age
- Bankruptcy
- Real estate
- Corporate affiliations (*if they are listed as an officer*)
- Address summary (*current and previous, neighborhood profile*)
- Liens and judgments
- UCC Filings
- Cell phone listing
- Ranking in corporation (*if affiliated*)
- Driver's license information

- Vehicle description
- Voter registration
- Possible criminal records
- Sexual offenses
- Permits (*hunting, gun, etc.*)
- People (*not relatives*) associated with subject
- Possible relatives summary

67. Corporate affiliations

If the report lists the person as a member of a corporation, dig deeper. The Secretary of State (SOS) keeps this information. You can call them directly or check their website by searching "Secretary of (*your state*)." The website will have instructions how to search business records.

 BONUS ONLINE CONTENT: For Secretary of State information for your state, visit www.BeASmartClient.com.

On the SOS site, you may find:

- Business Name
- Trade Name or Trademark
- Registered Agent
- Reserved Name Holder

- Trade Name Registrant
- Trademark Registrant

If your case is against the owner of a business, the person listed as the Registered Agent of the business would be the person to be served with a subpoena or summons. If the owner is listed as the registered agent for a business, perform a separate search of <u>only</u> registered agents to see if the owner is an agent for other companies. This comes in handy if they are hard to serve because it may give you more options. *Remember, the more information you have on a person, the better.*

There may be other details listed. Be sure to keep copies of everything.

68. Real estate ownership
After you obtain the defendant's home address, check the assessor's records to see if they own their home. Some county assessors list this information on-line. If they do not or you cannot locate it, call your

county assessor to get ownership details on the property. Anyone making mortgage payments is required to carry homeowner's insurance. This could pay your medical and other expenses.

69. Renter's insurance

If the defendant rents, are they living in a large community? Many management companies require occupants to carry rental insurance which potentially could cover your medical, legal and other costs.

70. Social media

In addition to legal agencies, you can find personal information about people from their on-line sites such as Facebook, LinkedIn and Twitter.

71. Case information

Your attorney should keep you apprised of court dates pertaining to your case. You can also contact the court. Any document filed with the court lists the district where your case is filed. Give them your case number and they will give you court dates. Ask them if you can check your case information online. Some districts list case information on their website. You can plug in the case number and see the court docket.

72. Back-up plan

You may encounter resistance trying to obtain information. When Plan A fails, try Plan B. For instance, if a city employee balks at giving you what you need, contact the City Council. Why? The City Council acts as the city's general counsel (attorney) and can contact the City on your behalf.

Contact government agencies in person, if possible. Let them put a face to the voice. Phone calls are too easily dismissed.

73. Insurance problems

If you have problems with an insurance company, contact the local regulatory agency. States

closely regulate the personal injury
insurance industry. For example,
Indiana has a set number of days to
acknowledge and respond to any
communication. If the insurance
company fails, the state will
investigate and fine the company if
they are at fault. When you have an
issue with an insurance carrier,
contact the Division of Insurance (*or
whatever it is called in your state*).

74. Save your breath

When contacting large companies or
government agencies, speak to first-
tier employees only once. Request a
supervisor the second time.
Management can circumvent rules;
subordinates cannot.

75. Check the facts

Don't automatically take what
others say as the truth. They may
be making an educated guess or the
information they have may have
recently changed. Get confirmation
from a second source to verify the
information you have is correct.

DO YOU REMEMBER?

1. If your lawyer does not provide you with court dates, what is another way you can find out?

2. Who should you contact if the insurance company doesn't pay a claim?

3. What are four items about a company you can get from the Secretary of State?

4. Why is it a smart to double check research facts?

5. Name eight items in a background check.

9

▶ PERSONAL SELF CARE

You may wonder why this chapter is included in this book. Even with careful planning, things can go wrong and proceed slower than you anticipated. If you have a personal injury case, this could be the most important chapter to you. Everyone is unique and reacts in their own way. Don't compare your situation to any other. *Do what makes you feel good and/or heal the fastest.*

76. Accept help from others

You may be very independent, but this is a time when you should rely on others. Allow your family and friends to help. **Be flexible in your expectations of people.** Those who can help, will. Those who cannot, may disappear from your life.

77. Sense of humor

When things look bleak, a sense of humor is one of your best tools. Keep friends close who have a good sense of humor. The more you look for the funny angle, the easier it becomes to find it. It is true, laughter is the best medicine.

78. Focus on positive things

If you watch TV, steer clear of violent shows. Stick to funny, upbeat shows. If you like to read, choose light novels, nothing heavy. Visit museums, watch funny or light-hearted movies, eat good food. Do things that make you feel good. *Did you know it is impossible to have two opposing thoughts at the same time?* When you think uplifting thoughts, it is hard to have a depressing thought.

79. Be good to your body

After sustaining an injury, you may not feel hungry. But you need to help your body heal. Eat wholesome food and drink lots of water. Mix nutritious food (*feed the body*) with comfort food (*feed the mind*). If you are taking antibiotics, take probiotics to offset them. Check with your doctor first.

80. Therapy can help
If your emotions are running amok, get help. Don't feel like you have to tough it out by yourself. Sessions with a therapist may help.

81. Full disclosure
When prescribing medication, the doctor will ask about allergies, vitamins and other medications you take. The more you share, the better. For instance, do you use caffeine? Is your stomach sensitive? Do you have problems swallowing pills? Tell your doctor as much as you can to help them make informed decisions.

82. Alternative health can help
Self-hypnosis and Emotional Freedom Technique (EFT) are powerful tools. They can help you

gain control during stressful times by lowering blood pressure, reduce anxiety and speeding the recovery process. Search YouTube.com for EFT videos.

If surgery is required, ask the anesthesiologist or someone else who will be present during the operation to give you suggestions. You could also make a recording and ask to listen to it during surgery. When you are under anesthesia, anything you hear drops into your subconscious mind and the mind works on it to make it happen.

 BONUS ONLINE CONTENT: Visit www.SourceOfEnlightenment.com to read more on hypnosis and EFT and details on making your own surgery tape.

83. Medical assistants
Let doctors concentrate on taking care of your injury. Try not to take up their time with things that can be handled by others. A nurse can answer many questions. As was suggested for appointments with

lawyers, **take someone with you** on doctor visits whenever possible.

84. Similar situations

Seek out people who have experienced what you are going through. Look for support groups through your church, school, www.Meetups.com or other social groups. They can give you insight and empathize with you.

85. Regain your power

If you were in a car accident or suffered some other injury, return to the location (*if it is safe*) once you are mentally and physically able. Shut your eyes and imagine taking back any power you might have lost there. One aspect of experiencing trauma is the feeling of being helpless. Taking back your power is a way to feel strong again.

86. Help others

Is there some way to share your experience so others can benefit from your experience? Give talks, write articles or letter to the editor, call a radio show. This kind of action helps you regain control.

87. The "Big Picture"
It is normal to think "Why did this happen to me?" We like to have answers especially when something bad happens. You may never get an answer, but if you look for the bigger picture, it might make you feel better. How can you see the bigger picture?

Imagine it happened to someone else. Step back and imagine the situation through someone else's eyes. What exactly happened and how has their (your) life changed since the incident?

Remove all emotion. Look at the situation like an attorney would. Write it down as you remember it. Then delete all adjectives and adverbs until you have the bare bones of the situation.

What did you learn? What could you share with others to make someone else's life better? Share what you have learned. You will feel better for it and they will benefit from your experience.

DO YOU REMEMBER?

1. Name three things you can do that will make you feel better.

2. Why should you not compare yourself to others?

3. How can you see the "bigger picture"?

4. Why is it important to talk to others who have gone through the same thing?

10

►LEGAL TERMS

AKA, a/k/a, f/k/a - Also known as, formerly known as.

Arbitration - An out-of-court hearing in which a single person (*or panel of attorneys and non-attorneys*) not involved in the dispute will listen to you and your lawyer to help reach a solution. In binding arbitration you will have limited ability to appeal.

Attorney - A person legally appointed by another to act as his or her agent in the transaction of business, specifically one qualified and licensed to act for plaintiffs and defendants in legal proceedings.

Attorney (Litigation) represents clients who are suing or being sued (personal injury, civil and criminal matters).

Attorney (transactional) is one who specializes in areas of business law (contracts, real estate).

Calendar - To assign a case a courtroom, day and time. Also refers to noting due dates of action to be taken in a case.

Civil (Case) - The private rights and remedies of men, as members of the community.

Criminal (Case) - An action, suit, or cause instituted to punish an infraction of the criminal laws.

Contingency Fee - Payment for legal services that depends, or is contingent, upon there being some recovery or award in the case. The payment is then a percentage of the amount recovered.

Defendant - The person defending or denying; the party against whom relief or recovery is sought in an action or suit.

Deposition - The testimony of a witness reduced to writing by a duly-qualified officer and sworn to by the deponent (*person being questioned*).

Discovery - In a general sense, to learn which was previously unknown; the disclosure or coming to light of what was previously hidden.

Docket - An abbreviated formal record of the proceedings in a court of justice.

Due Diligence -To investigate and evaluate a business opportunity. A general duty to exercise care in any transaction.

Interrogatories - A set of written questions formally asked by one party to the opposing party.

Litigation - A contest in a court of justice, for the purpose of enforcing a right.

Litigator - Lawyer who specializes in criminal or civil litigation.

Make You Whole - This refers to doing what is needed to make restitution, or return the victim to a condition where as best as possible, they haven't lost anything.

Mediation - Friendly or diplomatic intervention, usually by consent or invitation for settling differences between persons, nations, etc.

MMI - Means "Maximum Medical Improvement," the point at which a medical provider determines a person's condition cannot be improved any further.

Opposing Counsel - Attorney for the other side.

Personal Injury - Personal injury law involves injury which is caused accidentally by another's failure to use reasonable care.

Petitioner - One who presents a petition to a court, officer, or legislative body.

Plaintiff - A person who brings an action; the party who complains or sues in a personal action and is named on the record.

Redacted - Censor or obscure text for legal or security purposes.

Restitution - The return of something to the owner or to the person entitled to possession. Compensation for loss.

Statute of Limitations - A federal or state law that restricts the time within which legal proceedings may be brought.

Timekeeper - A person who bills for their time on a case.

Tort - A wrong or wrongful act as distinguished from a contract.

Warrant - A document issued by a legal or government official which authorizes the police or some other body to make an arrest or search the premises.

Work Product - Memoranda, writings, notes, research, and confidential materials which a lawyer has developed while representing a client, especially in preparation for trial. These documents are not included when the file is given to the client at the conclusion of a case.

ABOUT THE AUTHOR

 Ellen Hughes started The McKee Company in 1992 as a publishing vehicle for her writings. The tagline has been updated to "An Idea Company" to reflect the diversity of products.

These products have received favorable reviews in *Readers Digest, Kiplinger Washington Letter, Denver Business Journal,* and other publications.

The McKee Company offers several products. Most notable are: 1) **Office Wizard** - software program which creates a personalized procedures and policy manual, 2) **Adventures With Natural Healing** - organizes 27 alternative health methods making it easy to choose which the right one, and 3) **Be A Smart Client** - teaches people how to be effective when dealing with legal matters.

www.TheMcKeeCompany.com.

CLIENT WORKBOOKS

Be A Smart **Client** is an excellent source of basic and specific information for those who find themselves needing an attorney. This book is unique in that it is written about how to <u>improve</u> the attorney/client relationship. To further help both parties, **Be A Smart Client** offers companion workbooks.

Client Workbooks are available to help the client record and organize their case details in one place. It is a valuable tool for both client and attorney. Each workbook covers a specific type of case and includes checklists, charts, tips, and suggestions for ease of use. It can help anyone Be A Smart Client.

For details on Client Workbooks, visit www.BeASmartClient.com/Workbook.

Current workbooks available:

Personal Injury
Estate Planning